AF226019

Meta-Postal Expression

Kent Zimmerman

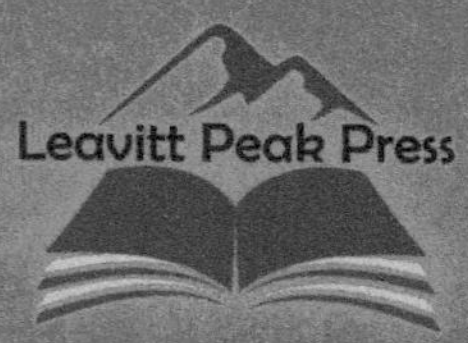

ISBN: 978-1-968970-43-7 (sc)
ISBN: 978-1-968970-44-4 (e)

Rev. date: 03/25/2026

Meta-Postal Expression are from hand painted 35mm slides on Mylar processed in digital format. The Expressions are created from studio characters are iconic components in audio-visual communications. Thank you Kodak, Bell and Howell, and Dolby sound. Play on!

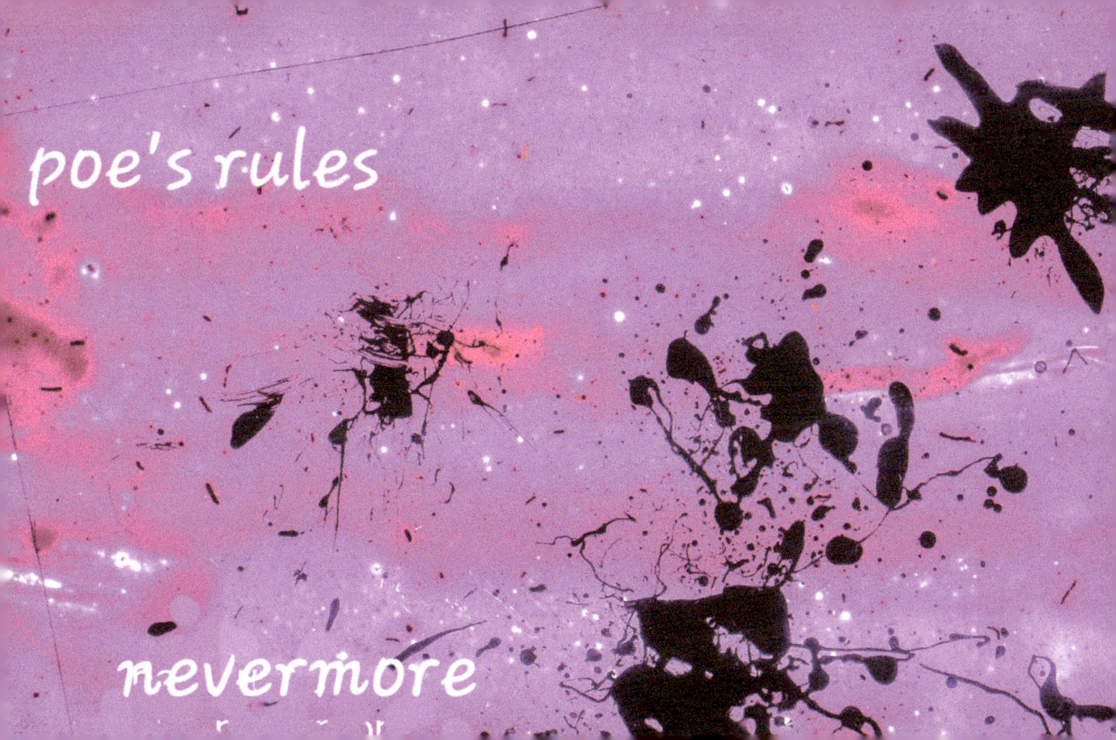
poe's rules
nevermore

Zimmerman: Meta-Postal Expression

Kent G Zimmerman

poe's rules nevermore

Hand Painted 35mm slides

Published by Leavitt Peak Press

WWW.LEAVITTPEAKPRESS.COM

1-888-549-098

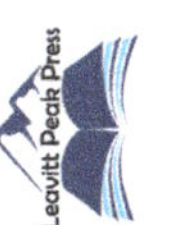

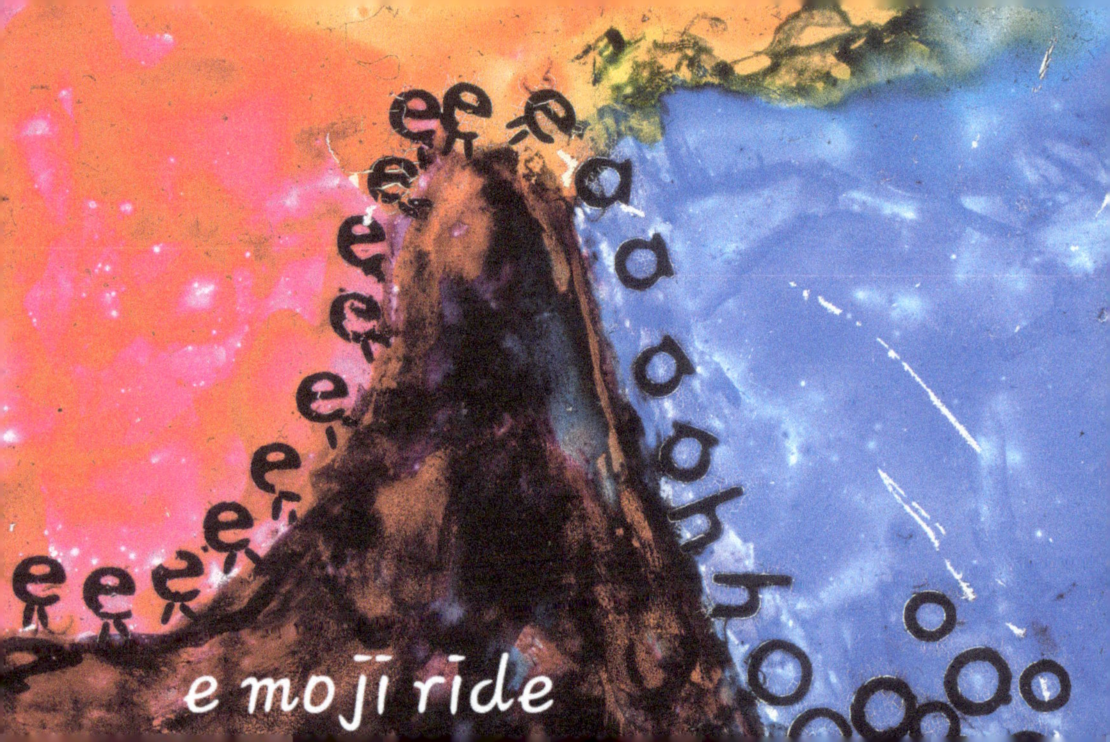
e moji ride

Zimmerman: Meta-Postal Expression

Kent G Zimmerman

emoji ride

Hand Painted 35mm slides

Published by Leavitt Peak Press

WWW.LEAVITTPEAKPRESS.COM

1-888-549-098

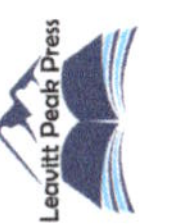

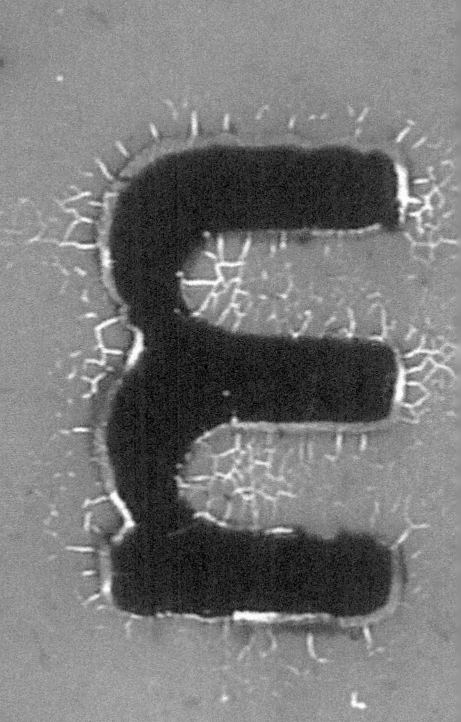

m black to blue

Zimmerman: Meta-Postal Expression

Kent G Zimmerman

m black to blue

Hand Painted 35mm slides

Published by Leavitt Peak Press

WWW.LEAVITTPEAKPRESS.COM

1-888-549-098

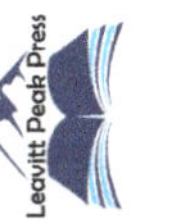

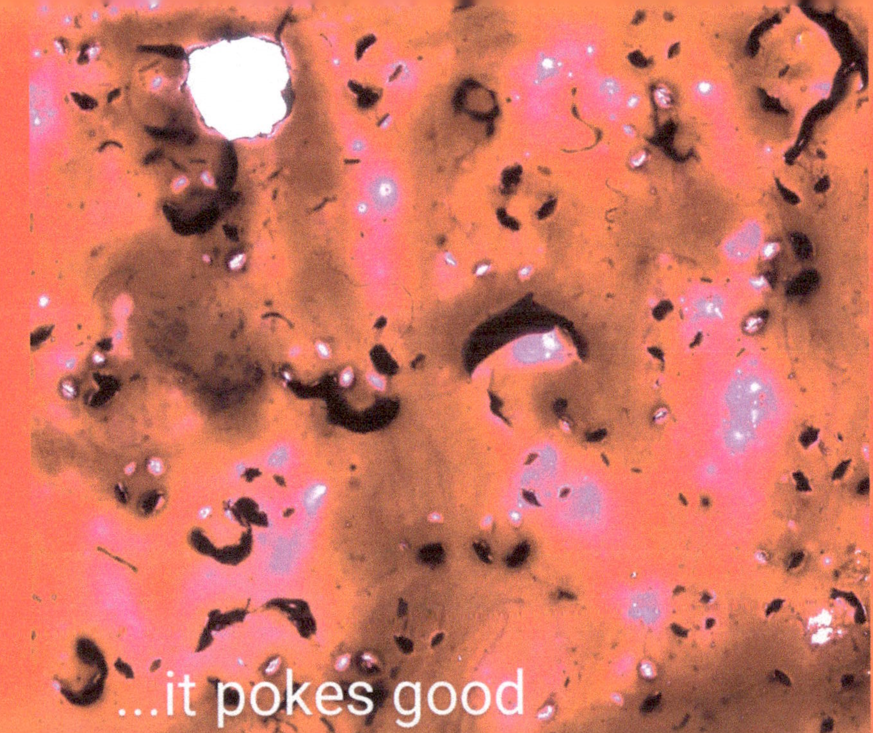
...it pokes good

Zimmerman: Meta-Postal Expression

Kent G Zimmerman

...it pokes good

Hand Painted 35mm slides

Published by Leavitt Peak Press

WWW.LEAVITTPEAKPRESS.COM

1-888-549-098

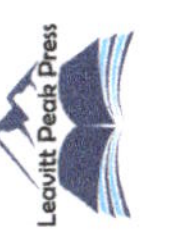

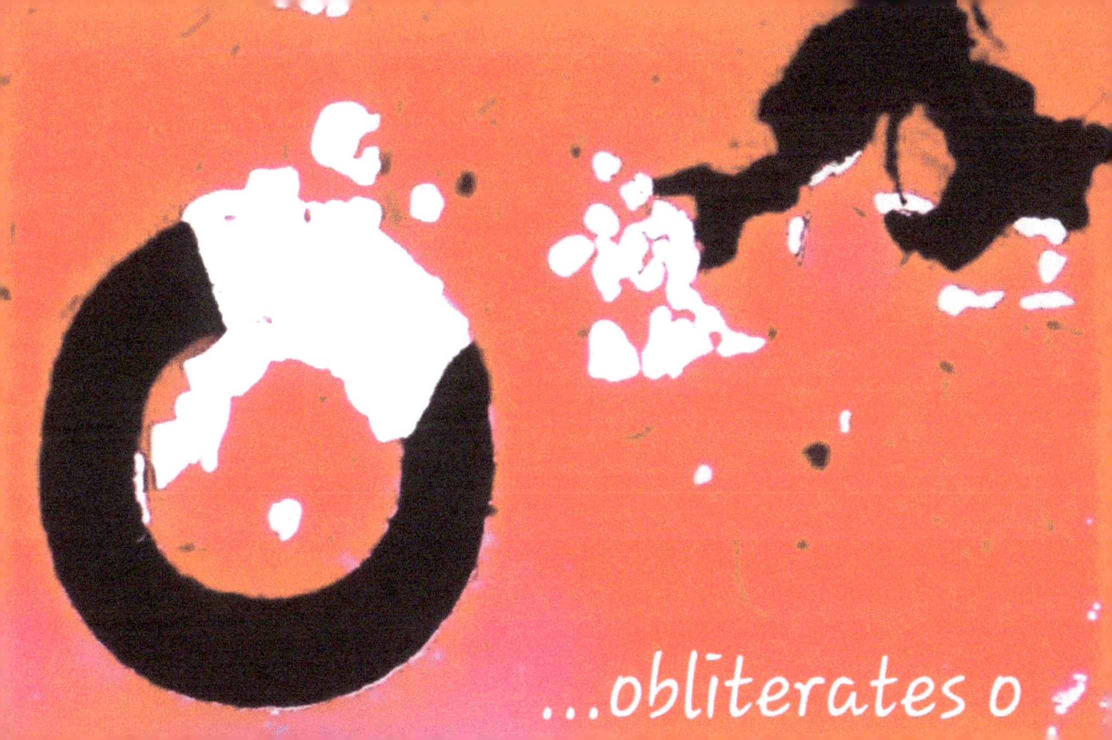
...obliterates o

Zimmerman: Meta-Postal Expression

Kent G Zimmerman

...obliterates o

Hand Painted 35mm slides

Published by Leavitt Peak Press

1-888-549-098

WWW.LEAVITTPEAKPRESS.COM

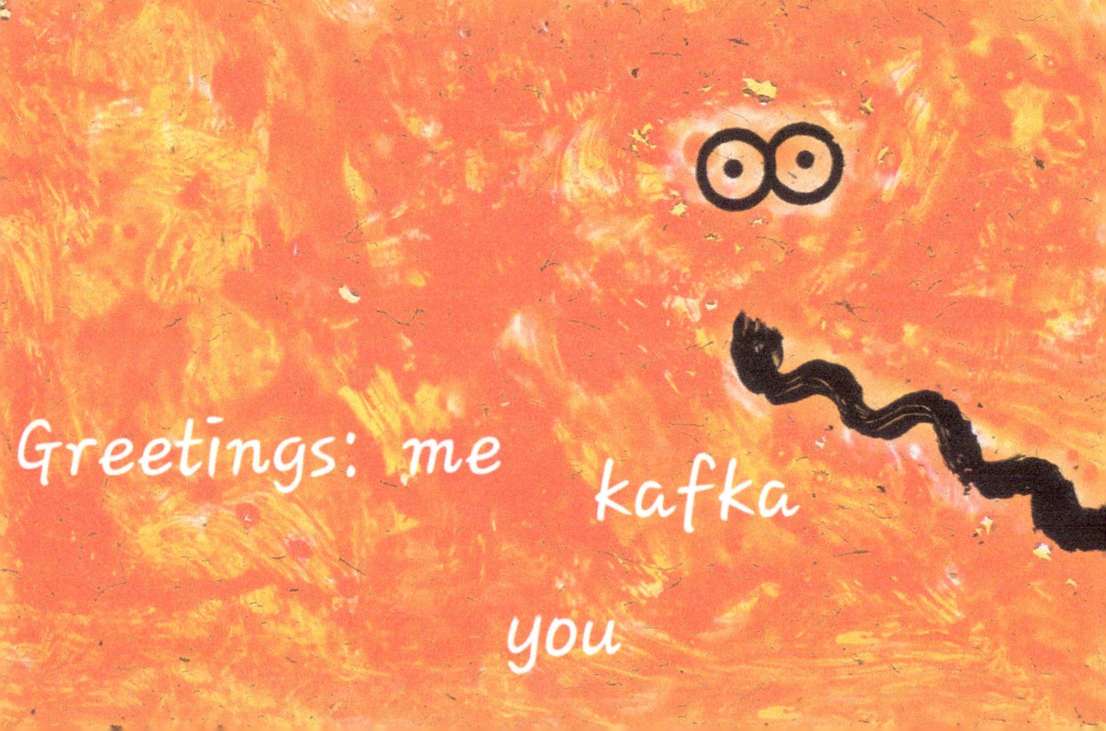
Greetings: me
kafka
you

Zimmerman: Meta-Postal Expression

Kent G Zimmerman

Greetings: me kafka you

Hand Painted 35mm slides

Published by Leavitt Peak Press

WWW.LEAVITTPEAKPRESS.COM

1-888-549-098

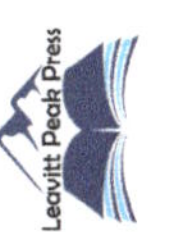

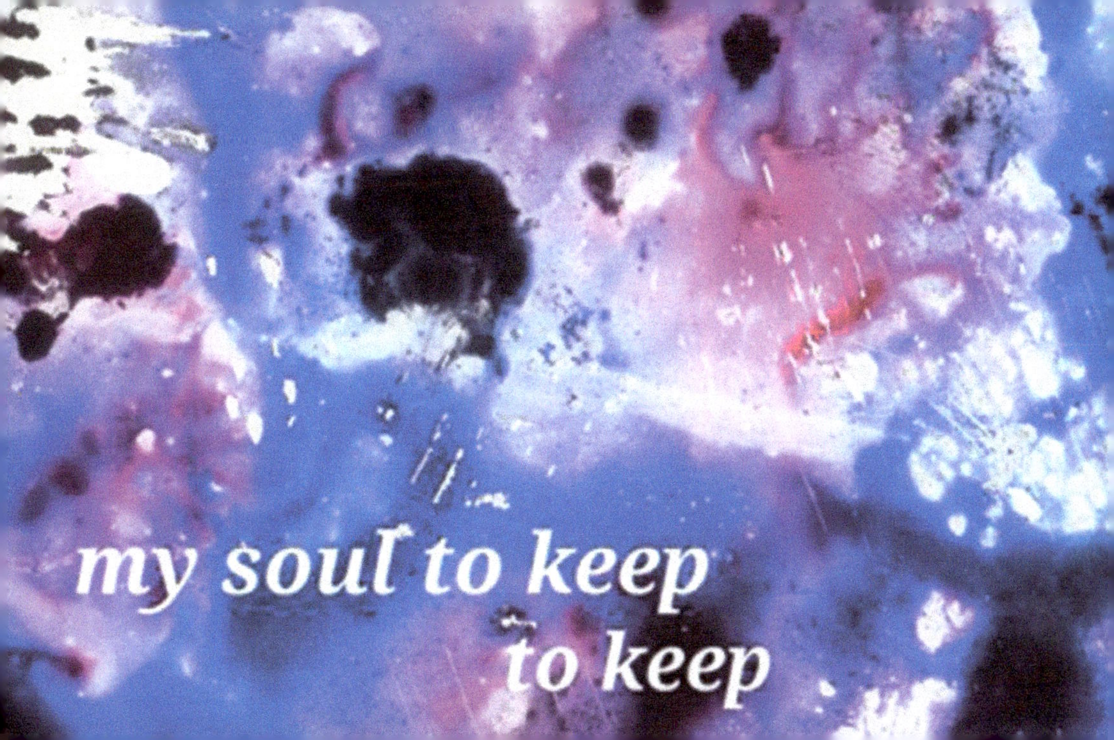
my soul to keep
to keep

Zimmerman: Meta-Postal Expression

Kent G Zimmerman

my soul to keep to keep

Hand Painted 35mm slides

Published by Leavitt Peak Press

WWW.LEAVITTPEAKPRESS.COM

1-888-549-098

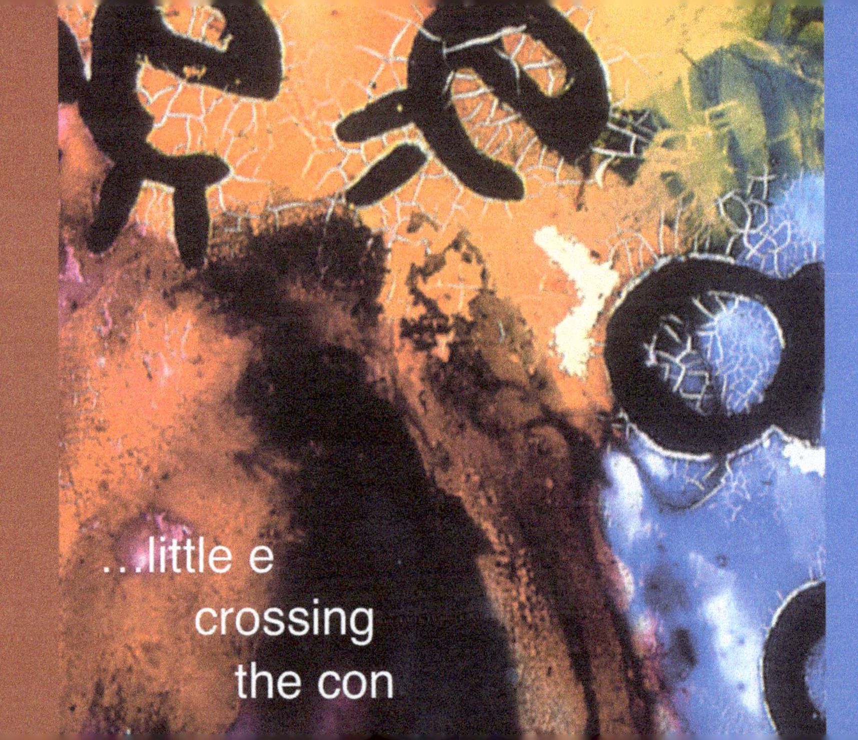
...little e
crossing
the con

Zimmerman: Meta-Postal Expression

Kent G Zimmerman

...little e crossing the con

Hand Painted 35mm slides

Published by Leavitt Peak Press

WWW.LEAVITTPEAKPRESS.COM

1-888-549-098

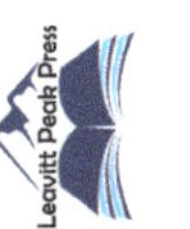
Leavitt Peak Press

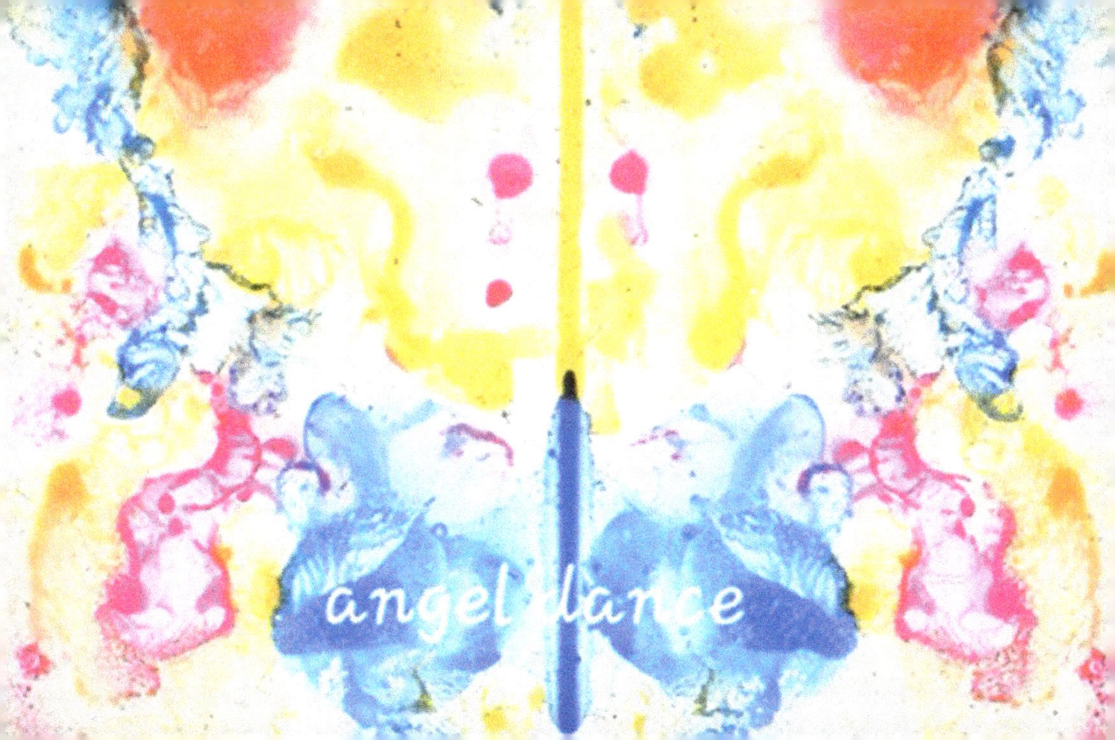
angel dance

Zimmerman: Meta-Postal Expression

Kent G Zimmerman

angel dance

Hand Painted 35mm slides

Published by Leavitt Peak Press

WWW.LEAVITTPEAKPRESS.COM

1-888-549-098

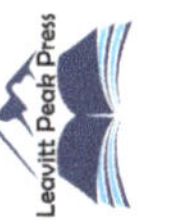

so spot out of ...

Zimmerman: Meta-Postal Expression

Kent G Zimmerman

so spot out of...

Hand Painted 35mm slides

Published by Leavitt Peak Press

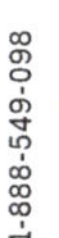

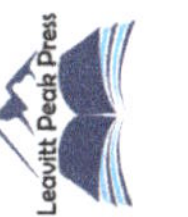

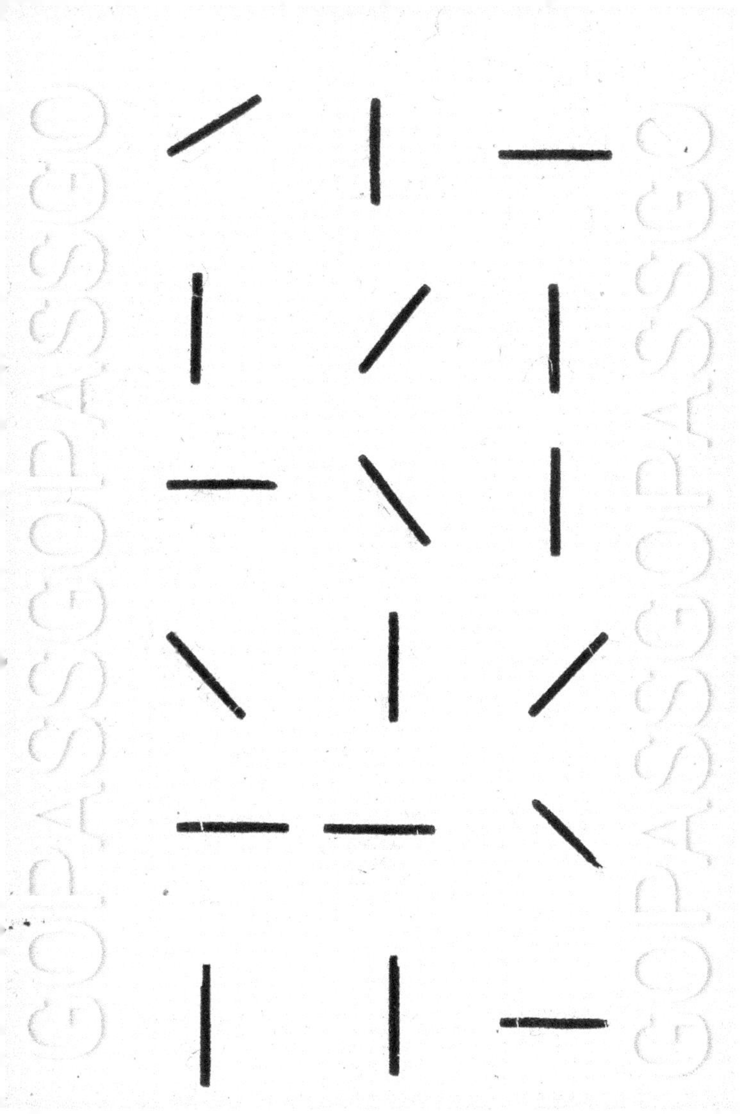

Zimmerman: Meta-Postal Expression

Kent G Zimmerman

GOPASSGOPASSGO

Hand Painted 35mm slides

Published by Leavitt Peak Press

WWW.LEAVITTPEAKPRESS.COM

1-888-549-098

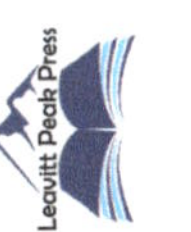

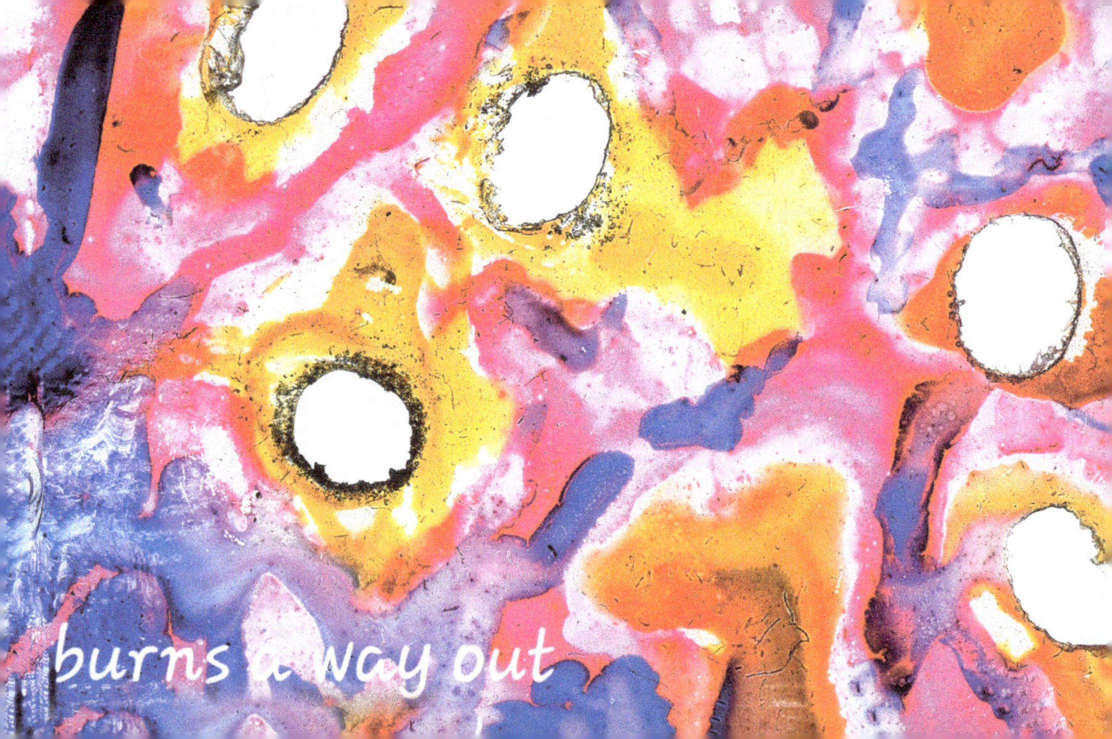
burns a way out

Zimmerman: Meta-Postal Expression

Kent G Zimmerman

burns a way out

Hand Painted 35mm slides

Published by Leavitt Peak Press

WWW.LEAVITTPEAKPRESS.COM

1-888-549-098

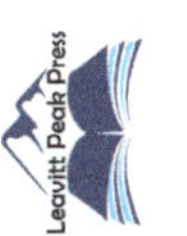

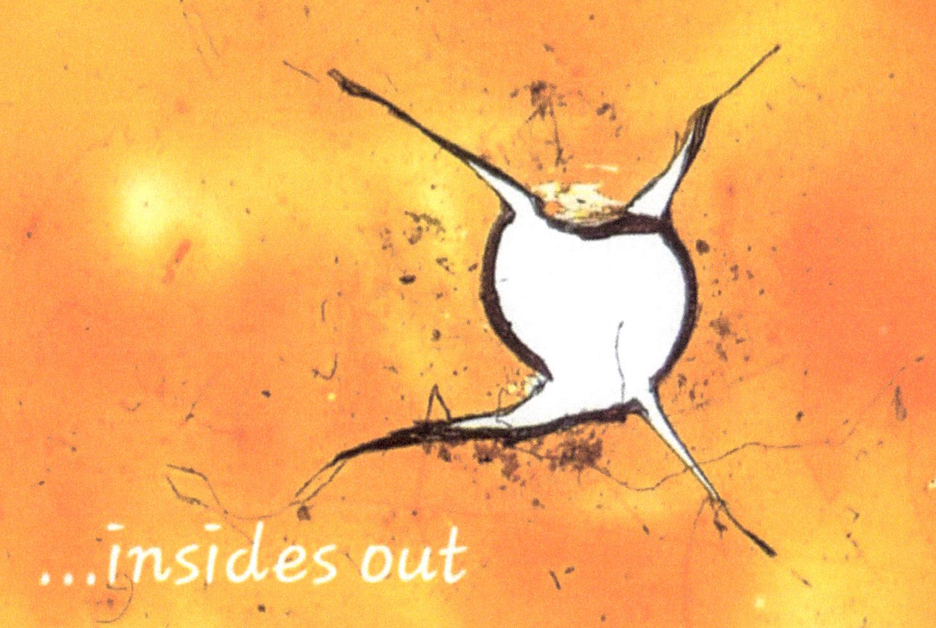
...insides out

Zimmerman: Meta-Postal Expression

Kent G Zimmerman

...inside out

Hand Painted 35mm slides

Published by Leavitt Peak Press

WWW.LEAVITTPEAKPRESS.COM

1-888-549-098

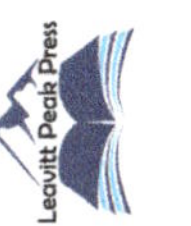

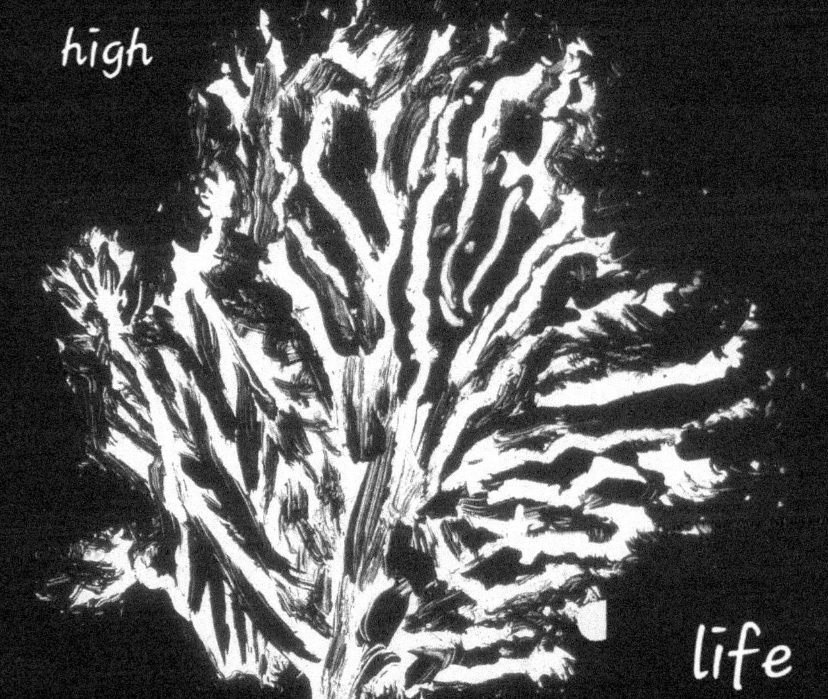
high
life

Zimmerman: Meta-Postal Expression

Kent G Zimmerman

high life

Hand Painted 35mm slides

Published by Leavitt Peak Press

WWW.LEAVITTPEAKPRESS.COM

1-888-549-098

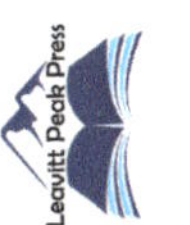

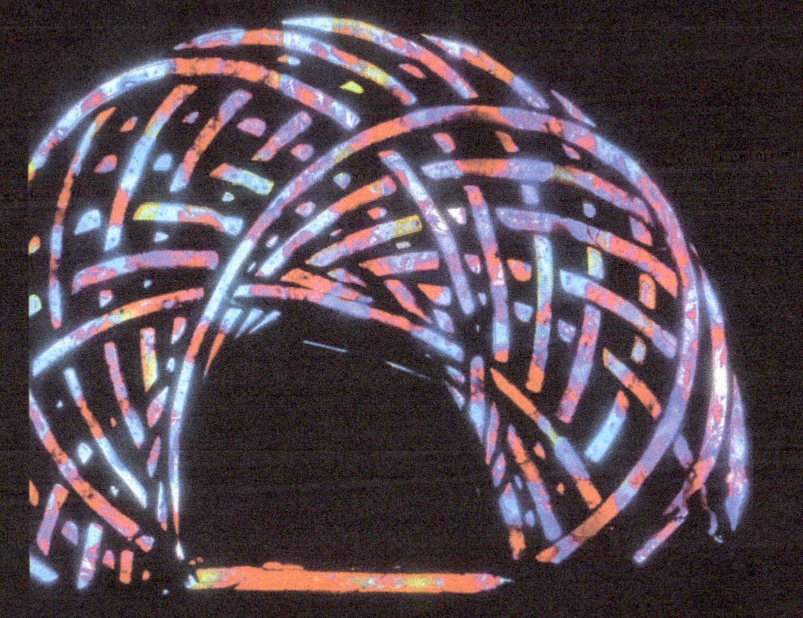

confabulist psalm

Zimmerman: Meta-Postal Expression

Kent G Zimmerman

confabulist psalm

Hand Painted 35mm slides

Published by Leavitt Peak Press

WWW.LEAVITTPEAKPRESS.COM

1-888-549-098

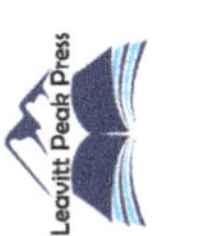

good night

Zimmerman: Meta-Postal Expression

Kent G Zimmerman

good night

Hand Painted 35mm slides

Published by Leavitt Peak Press

WWW.LEAVITTPEAKPRESS.COM

1-888-549-098

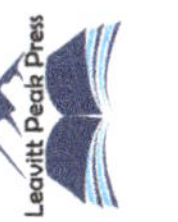